D1327478

DALL SHEEP MIGRATION

BY REBECCA HIRSCH

The Child's World®

Published by The Child's World®
1980 Lookout Drive • Mankato, MN 56003-1705
800-599-READ • www.childsworld.com

ACKNOWLEDGMENTS
The Child's World®: Mary Berendes, Publishing Director
Content Consultant: Dr. Tanya Dewey,
    University of Michigan Museum of Zoology
The Design Lab: Design and production
Red Line Editorial: Editorial direction

PHOTO CREDITS
Eric Gagneraud/Dreamstime, cover (bottom), 2–3; Dreamstime, cover (top),
1, back cover; Images in the Wild/iStockphoto, 4, 9, 16; The Design Lab, 7;
TT Photo/Shutterstock Images, 8; Marc Herrmann/Shutterstock Images, 10;
Don Handley/Bigstock, 11; Monique Vorstenbosch/iStockphoto, 12; Richard
L. Carlson/Fotolia, 14–15; Richard Larson/iStockphoto, 18; Images in the
Wild/Dreamstime, 19; Lilac Mountain/Shutterstock Images, 20–21; Matthew
Jacques/Shutterstock Images, 23; Sam Chadwick/Shutterstock Images,
24–25; Paul Tessier/iStockphoto, 27; Fred Lord/Bigstock, 28–29

Design elements: Dreamstime

ISBN 9781609736194
LCCN 2011940062

Printed in the United States of America

ABOUT THE AUTHOR: Rebecca Hirsch, PhD, is the author of several nonfiction books for children. A former biologist, she writes for children and young adults about science and the natural world. She lives with her husband and three daughters in State College, Pennsylvania.

TABLE OF CONTENTS

DALL SHEEP

Dall sheep live in some of the rockiest land in North America. Dall sheep are mountain sheep. They are at home on **ledges** and steep cliffs. But the sheep cannot find everything they need to live in one place. They travel with the seasons. Dall sheep migrate up and down the mountains. They climb to different heights in different seasons. This is called **altitudinal** migration.

The Dall sheep's lifetime journey is their migration. This is when an animal moves from one **habitat** to another. Migrations happen for many reasons. Some animals move to be in warmer weather where there is more food. There they can reproduce or have their babies. And these migrations can be long distances, such as hundreds of miles in the ocean. Or they can be short distances, like the Dall sheep's journey.

Dall sheep migrate up and down the mountains where they live.

MIGRATION MAP

Dall sheep live in the mountains of Alaska and northwestern Canada. Some live on Mount McKinley. This is the tallest mountain in North America.

In spring, the sheep start up the mountain. The females find rocky cliffs to give birth to their lambs. Dall sheep spend summers high on the slopes. When winter comes, they climb back down the mountain where it is warmer. They change **climates** by moving on the mountain.

Dall sheep live in parts of Canada and Alaska.

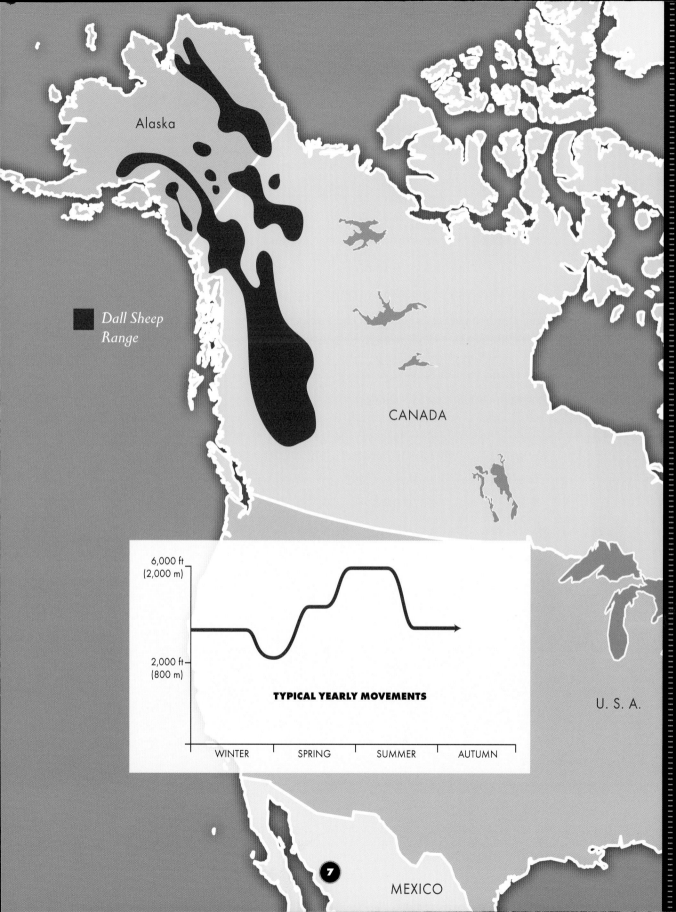

Alaska

Dall Sheep
Range

CANADA

U. S. A.

MEXICO

TYPICAL YEARLY MOVEMENTS

6,000 ft
(2,000 m)

2,000 ft
(800 m)

WINTER   SPRING   SUMMER   AUTUMN

MASTER CLIMBERS

Dall sheep are great climbers. They are quick and can easily go up steep cliffs and rocky mountains. The sheep jump from ledge to ledge. They can climb nearly straight up and down on the rock. They rarely fall. Their toes can grip the rocks well. The sheep climb to reach the high meadows. These meadows are full of food. The sheep also climb to escape wolves and grizzly bears. These **predators** rarely go as high as the sheep.

Dall sheep eat grasses and other plants that grow on the mountains. Their strong lips and tongues grab and tear the plants. Their flat teeth grind their food as they chew. They swallow the tough and chewy food. Then they bring the food up again into the mouth. They chew the food a second time.

Dall sheep climb very rocky land.

The male sheep are called rams. The female sheep are called ewes. Both rams and ewes have horns. The ewes have horns that are short and pointed. The rams have horns that grow in a spiral. As the rams grow older, the horns form a circle. Dall sheep horns grow from spring to fall. Then they stop growing in winter. This makes rings. The rings are spaced along the outside of the horn. You can tell the age of the sheep by counting the rings.

The mountain meadows have plenty of food for the sheep.

Dall sheep live in groups called bands. The rams live in one band. The ewes and lambs live in another. The male and female bands mix together in November and December to mate. Then they separate again.

Rings form on the spiral horns of the sheep.

A DALL SHEEP'S HORNS ARE MADE OF BONE. KERATIN COVERS THE BONE. KERATIN IS ALSO IN HUMAN FINGERNAILS.

In every band, each sheep has its place. The oldest animal in each band is the **dominant** sheep. This animal is the leader. In male bands, the rams fight to become leaders. Older rams have bigger horns. They almost always win. They become the leaders in their band. The other sheep know to follow the leaders.

Dall sheep live in bands.

THINHORN SHEEP

Dall sheep live on mountains in the far north. Stone sheep live in mountains south of where the Dall sheep live. Both are thinhorn sheep. Dall sheep and stone sheep are the same **species**. They look almost the same. But, Dall sheep have snowy white coats. Stone sheep have black, brown, or gray coats.

Why do Dall sheep and stone sheep look different? Thousands of years ago, great sheets of ice called **glaciers** covered the land. Huge amounts of water were frozen in glaciers and sea levels were low. A wide bridge of land connected Alaska with Russia. Wild sheep walked across this land to North America.

In their new home, the sheep spread out. Some settled on the snowy mountains in the far north. Others settled in forested mountains in the south.

Stone sheep are the same species as Dall sheep.

RAM'S HORNS REACH A FULL
CIRCLE IN ABOUT EIGHT YEARS.
THE LENGTH OF THE CURVE
OF A RAM'S HORN CAN BE
LONGER THAN 3 FEET (1 M).

Some scientists think that the sheep changed over time. It was easy for predators to see dark sheep on snowy mountains. White sheep blended in better. They could hide better from predators. As time passed, only the white sheep stayed alive. They had lambs with white coats. Today these white sheep are called Dall sheep. Just as the Dall sheep became white, the sheep to the south began to have dark coats. This helped them blend in with their forest home. Today they are called stone sheep.

Stone and Dall sheep's coats blend with the places where they live.

UP THE MOUNTAIN

The spring sun rises over the mountains. The snow begins to melt. And Dall sheep start to move. The animals have spent the winter low on the mountain in places with less snow. The sheep move uphill. There the first spring plants are poking out of the ground. The sheep graze their way back up the mountain. They follow the melting snow and eat fresh green plants. After a long winter, the hungry sheep want to fill up on food.

The dominant sheep in each band leads the way. It guides the others along trails the sheep have used for years. The sheep are careful. They do not wander from the routes they know are safe. They will not explore unknown canyons or valleys. Wolves and coyotes could be waiting for them.

In May or June, each pregnant ewe leaves her band. She finds a cliff to have her lamb. She chooses the cliff carefully. She wants one that is steep and rocky. Predators cannot follow her there.

In spring Dall sheep move up the mountain again.

Ewes give birth to their lambs on cliffs.

The new lambs weigh 6 to 9 pounds (2 to 4 kg) at birth. The ewe and her lamb bond. They learn each other's smell. They know the sound of each other's **bleating**. The mother feeds the lamb her milk. The lamb grows quickly. Soon it moves around on the rocky cliffs and nibbles the plants. In a few days, the ewe and her lamb are ready to join the band.

The band is now filled with lambs. They travel along paths to **mineral** licks. These are places where the ground is rich in minerals. The sheep eat the soil. They fill up on **nutrients** they cannot get from their food. The sheep stay for a few days. Then they continue climbing the mountain.

SUMMER MEADOWS

In summer the sun shines day and night. The meadows high on the mountains fill with food. The sheep climb higher and higher. There are few other grazing animals so high on the mountain. The sheep get the meadows mostly to themselves.

In the summer, there are plenty of green grasses and plants for the sheep to eat.

Dall sheep have shed their thick winter coats. They now have white summer fur. It helps them in the bright sunshine. A dark coat would take in heat. The white coat **reflects** the sunlight. It keeps them cool.

Summer is a time for raising lambs. The lambs run and play together in the meadows. Playing helps them learn their place in the group. Lambs have a lot to learn in their first year of life. They must learn to find food. They must learn the migration routes. And they must learn how to escape danger.

Summer is also a time to prepare for the long winter. The sheep graze heavily. They must build up fat for winter. Rams need to store enough energy for the winter and the coming **rut**. Ewes need to gain weight to give birth next spring. Lambs must eat enough to grow quickly before winter. By fall the lambs will weigh ten times as much as they did at birth.

Playing helps lambs learn their places in the group.

FALL AND THE RUT

The days grow shorter as summer ends. Icy winds blow across the mountains. The food in the meadows begins to run out. The sheep cannot survive the winter here. They cannot find food through the thick snow. The sheep move back down the mountain. They follow worn trails and graze on the way.

Fall is the time to mate. All year the rams fight to see which male is stronger. The rut is coming soon. So the fights become wilder. The mountains echo with the sound of horns crashing together.

Two rams push and shove each other. Then the two animals back up. They run toward each other and clash horn to horn. Fights can last for hours. It ends when one ram is tired, hurt, or finally gives in. The winning males can mate with ewes. Young rams do not breed until their horns grow large enough to win these battles.

Rams fight each other during the rut.

RAMS ARE BUILT FOR
THESE BATTLES. THEY
HAVE A DOUBLE LAYER OF
BONE ON THEIR SKULLS.

THE COLD WINTER

In winter the mountain weather is very cold and windy. Dall sheep live lower on the mountain. The snowfall is lighter. But it is still hard to live low on the slopes. Snow and ice cover the ground. Freezing winds blow. It is dark.

Dall sheep have two layers of fur. This helps them stay warm in the cold. A woolly layer keeps the animal warm. Long, hollow guard hairs cover the wool. Each guard hair is filled with air. The hair forms a kind of blanket that keeps out the cold. The sheep look big in their thick winter coats.

Winter life is tough. The sheep search for patches of grass where the snow is light. They paw through the snow to find the plants underneath. They look for windy areas. The wind blows the snow away. The winter diet is mostly frozen grasses and plant stems. The sheep begin to eat other plants, such as **lichens**, willows, and mosses. Sometimes freezing rain covers the snow. It forms a hard crust of ice on top. The sheep cannot paw through to the plants underneath. They must live off their fat. They grow thinner as the winter passes.

Winters are cold, snowy, and windy on the mountain.

Winter is a dangerous time for Dall sheep. Some lambs may be too small to make it through the winter. Dominant rams who win the rut, lose a lot of fat. They may not have enough left to get through the winter. And if ewes grow too thin, they may not be able to give birth in the spring.

MOUNTAIN DANGERS

A Dall sheep's life is filled with danger. Golden eagles can swoop down and catch lambs that stray. Wolves, coyotes, and grizzly bears can attack the band.

The sheep's white fur helps them hide. The sheep blend into the white snow. They can be hard for predators to spot.

Dall sheep have senses to alert them to predators. They have big eyes on the sides of their heads. Their eyesight is as strong as a person's eyes looking through binoculars. They have noses that sniff the air for the scent of predators. Their large ears move front to back. The sheep listen from all sides.

Living in a group also helps the sheep. They have many eyes watching for predators. If a predator is near, the sheep may run. Or they may snort, paw the ground, and bow their heads. Sometimes the sheep stand close together. They face their horns out. They can fight a predator as a group. But the high rocks keep them safe better than anything else. They climb to places where predators cannot follow.

Males and females often live in different places on the mountains. Females must keep their lambs safe. They will go to high rocky spots. The males are more able to fight a predator. They can live in lower spots.

Dall sheep have very good eyesight.

HELP FOR DALL SHEEP

For thousands of years, native peoples in the Arctic hunted Dall sheep. They ate the animal's meat. They made blankets, jackets, and clothes from their coats. They made dishes and ladles from the horns.

In the 1900s, many people moved into the far north. They were looking for gold. The white settlers hunted the sheep. So many sheep were killed that the Dall sheep **population** fell.

Today there 60,000 to 90,000 Dall sheep in Canada and Alaska. People still hunt Dall sheep, but there are laws to stop too many sheep from being killed.

Most Dall sheep live in areas with few roads. They are far from people. Dall sheep usually stay on one mountain range. They follow the same routes from year to year. If humans build roads, mines, or camps on the range, the sheep can be slow to leave. They may stay even when the area is no longer safe for them.

Scientists study Dall sheep to understand and keep them safe from people. They fly airplanes over the places where Dall sheep live. They count the animals. They also count lambs. This gives the scientists an idea of the numbers of Dall sheep. Scientists also track

Dall sheep with radio collars. A few animals are caught and collars are put around their necks. The animals are weighed and the rings on their horns are counted. Then the sheep are let go. Scientists learn where the sheep travel in different seasons.

Today people work to keep Dall sheep and their habitat safe. If many Dall sheep die in bad winters, hunting may be closed for a few years. The population has a chance to grow again. Scientists may set wildfires in some areas. These fires help certain plants grow. They provide food for sheep. Scientists hope these efforts will help Dall sheep continue to live and migrate up and down mountains.

Alaska's Denali National Park is a place kept aside for Dall sheep and other animals.

DENALI NATIONAL PARK AND PRESERVE IN ALASKA WAS STARTED AS A RESERVE FOR DALL SHEEP. TODAY THE PARK COVERS NEARLY 6 MILLION ACRES (2.5 MILLION HECTARES).

TYPES OF MIGRATION

Different animals migrate for different reasons. Some move because of the climate. Some travel to find food or a mate. Here are the different types of animal migration:

Seasonal migration: This type of migration happens when the seasons change. Most animals migrate for this reason. Other types of migration, such as altitudinal and latitudinal, may also include seasonal migration.

Latitudinal migration: When animals travel north and south, it is called latitudinal migration. Doing so allows animals to change the climate where they live.

Altitudinal migration: This migration happens when animals move up and down mountains. In summer, animals can live higher on a mountain. During the cold winter, they move down to lower and warmer spots.

Reproductive migration: Sometimes animals move to have their babies. This migration may keep the babies safer when they are born. Or babies may need a certain habitat to live in after birth.

Nomadic migration: Animals may wander from place to place to find food in this type of migration.

Complete migration: This type of migration happens when animals are finished mating in an area. Then almost all of the animals leave the area. They may travel more than 15,000 miles (25,000 km) to spend winters in a warmer area.

Partial migration: When some, but not all, animals of one type move away from their mating area, it is partial migration. This is the most common type of migration.

Irruptive migration: This type of migration may happen one year, but not the next. It may include some or all of a type of animal. And the animal group may travel short or long distances.

> SOMETIMES ANIMALS NEVER COME BACK TO A PLACE WHERE THEY ONCE LIVED. THIS CAN HAPPEN WHEN HUMANS OR NATURE DESTROY THEIR HABITAT. FOOD, WATER, OR SHELTER MAY BECOME HARD TO FIND. OR A GROUP OF ANIMALS MAY BECOME TOO LARGE FOR AN AREA. THEN THEY MUST MOVE TO FIND FOOD.

GLOSSARY

altitudinal (AL-ti-tude-uh-nal): Altitudinal is something that is done from different heights above the ground. Dall sheep are altitudinal migrators.

bleating (BLEET-ing): Goats and sheep makes sounds called bleating. Lambs listen for their mothers' bleating.

climates (KLYE-mitz): Climates are the usual weather in different places. There are different climates at different heights of the mountain.

dominant (DOM-uh-nuhnt): A dominant animal has the most power in a group. Rams fight to show which is the dominant animal.

glaciers (GLAY-shurz): Glaciers are huge sheets of ice that cover mountain valleys and areas by Earth's poles. Glaciers may have kept stone and Dall sheep apart for many years.

habitat (HAB-uh-tat): A habitat is a place that has the food, water, and shelter an animal needs to survive. The Dall sheep live in a mountain habitat.

keratin (CARE-uh-tin): Keratin is a protein found in horns, hair, human fingernails, and other things. Keratin is in a Dall sheep's horns.

ledges (LEJ-ez): Ledges are narrow shelves on the sides of mountains. Lambs are born on ledges.

lichens (LYE-kenz): Lichens are a flat plant that grows on rocks and trees. In the cold winter, Dall sheep eat lichens.

mineral (MIN-ur-uhl): A mineral is something found in nature that is not an animal or plant, such as salt and copper. Dall sheep need minerals in the soil.

nutrients (NOO-tree-untz): Nutrients are things that people, animals, and plants need to stay alive. The meadows provide nutrients for the sheep.

population (pop-yuh-LAY-shuhn): A population is all the animals of one type that live in the same area. Very cold winters can make the Dall sheep population fall.

predators (PRED-uh-turs): Predators are animals that hunt and eat other animals. Climbing helps the sheep escape predators.

reflects (ri-FLEKTZ): Light reflects when it bounces off an object. White fur reflects the sunshine.

reserve (ri-ZURV): A reserve is a place that is set aside to keep animals and plants safe. There is a reserve for Dall sheep in Alaska.

rut (RUHT): The rut is the time when animals mate. Rams fight during the rut.

species (SPEE-sheez): A species is a group of animals that are similar in certain ways. Dall and stone sheep are the same species.

FURTHER INFORMATION

Books

Gordon, Sharon. *Mountain Animals*. New York: Benchmark Books, 2008.

Kalman, Bobbie. *Baby Animals in Mountain Habitats*. New York: Crabtree Publishing, 2011.

Lang, Audrey. *Baby Mountain Sheep*. Markham, Ontario: Fitzhenry and Whiteside, 2007.

Richardson, Gillian. *Mountain Extremes*. New York: Crabtree Publishing, 2009.

Web Sites

Visit our Web site for links about Dall sheep migration: *childsworld.com/links*

Note to Parents, Teachers, and Librarians:

We routinely verify our Web links to make sure they are safe and active sites. So encourage your readers to check them out!

INDEX